Tom has set up a train track in his bedroom. It goes all round the floor and under his bed.

He connects two trucks to his green train. Then he pushes it round the track.

Bella comes to play. 'Please can I push a train round the track?' asks Bella.

Tom lets Bella have his red train. He lets her push it round the track.

Bella pushes the red train into the long green tunnel. Oh no! It stops in the tunnel.

'Tom, my train is stuck in the tunnel,' says Bella. 'I can't get it out.'

'Watch this,' says Tom. He gives his green train a big push into the tunnel.

Crash! Bang! Out comes the red train. A truck comes with it. Oh! Charlie is in the truck.